Wandering Musings

Jennifer Seal

Presentation by *BookLeaf Publishing*

Web: www.bookleafpub.com

E-mail: info@bookleafpub.com

ISBN: 9789357444866

First edition 2022

DEDICATION

This collection is dedicated to my grandparents.
I miss all of you every single day and I hope
that you are proud of me and what I have
accomplished.

ACKNOWLEDGEMENT

My parent's never once have failed to encourage me to take every step and express myself. Without them I wouldn't have the courage to take the chances I do and become the person I am.

Thrill of the Race

Burning.
Stretching.
Pulling.
Pushing.

Feet Pounding.
Out on the push down.
In as you lift the lead foot.
Hold it then repeat.

Eyes up
Watching the world pass.
Eyes down
Checking the ground.

Breathing deep.
Filling the lungs;
Pushing yourself harder.
The finish line is coming.

The sound rises around you,
The cheering and clapping.
You let it lift you;
Draw it in and use it.

Harder you push,
Digging deep for every step.
Grinding it out,
Fighting for every breath.

Soft sponge meets your feet.
So different from concrete.
A grin crosses your face.
Another race done.

Whiskey Dreams

Amber gold glistening in glass.
Slipping softly over crystal rocks.
Notes of sweet smokey wood.
Hints of the building blocks.
The flavor strongly withstood,
All attempts to drown it out.
Peach and apple sliding betwixt the lips.
Essence of fruit though the drought.
Delighting the tongue's tips.
Only the hardiest souls can give it a pass.

Beautiful Dancer

Light and graceful on your feet,
Turning, spinning, quickly you glide
You know out here you cannot hide
Out here on this frozen sheet.

Flashing bases show your moves
A curved edge leads the way
Your stick puts the puck in play
Jumping slightly as it hits the icy groves.

With a grunt you feel your breath leave
Shoving off the boards you spin
Your cousin snickers, on the ice he is no kin
Smirking, a trap you begin to weave.

Intercepting a pass the puck is yours
With a show of finesse your down the ice
Your muscles burning as you pay the price
For a chance to score any player endures

Its like a dance out there in the snow
A beautiful ballet of ice and steel
Laughter pouring for the, alive is how you feel.
Even though it is nearly ten below.

With practiced hands you line it up
A powerful thrust of the hands makes the shot
Long hanging seconds pass until it finds the spot
A yell comes forth, in your mind at least you've
won the Cup.

Baseball Blues

It's winter time again
And I got them old baseball blues.
It's football season you say
But I must confess I got them old baseball blues.
Who cares about basketball,
Or football or hockey?
Winter sports have nothing on the spring.
The smell of the grass and dirt
The shining green grass waving
Beyond the perfectly raked diamond of brown.
Gleaming white bases spread 90 feet apart.
Hot dogs and beer perfuming the air
Cotton candy and popcorn close behind
I can't wait for spring to come again.
Then I can chase away these old baseball blues.

Silver

I wear silver facing out.
I want to wear it facing in.
I want to say you are mine.
I want you to say I am yours.
I want to feel your love.
I want you to feel mine.

I wear silver facing out.
I want to wear it facing in.
I think about you constantly.
I think you might be perfect
 not in form, but for me.
I think we could be together.

I wear silver facing out.
I want to wear it facing in.
I want to spend time with you.
I want to spend my life with you.
I only want to be with you.
I want to wear the silver facing in.

Grief

Some days it wells up inside
Some days it sits as a hard ball
Some days it is buried deep
Some days it runs molten hot
The pain of missing you
It never really ends once it begins.

A tidal wave of grief comes
Crashing down it smothers me
Gasping for breath
Tears streaming down my face
Pain screaming in my heart
Exploding in my mind

A ball of sadness sits in my gut
Deep in the pit of my stomach
Filling me up
Food tastes like ash
Barely any needed to make me full
All I can feel is the grief.

No matter where I go or do
I feel like I'm dreaming
Missing you swamps over me
Taking over every part of my soul.

An almost physical manifestation
In the gasping for breath.

It will get better they say
One day it won't hurt so much
Some days I might even forget
Forget you aren't around anymore
Forget that I used to always need you,
But that seems so unlikely.

One foot in front of the other
Step by step and day by day
Living moment to moment
Then minute by minute.
Never let the grief win.
I live now for us both.

Fire and Ash

Dulled muted plummage
Head curled towards its breast
Weariness in every line
A faded, broken, dying body.
A mournful trill fills the air
Solitary note held for long seconds.
The air itself seems to say:
Farewell, my friend, farewell.

Flames rise up from nowhere
Whooshing over the weakened body
Consuming It in a blaze of color
Rich red, firey orange, glittering yellow
All twining together
A riotous, vacuous huge of crackling fire.
Just as suddenly it is gone.

A pile of slightly smoldering ash
Grey where once the colors flew
A mound where once there was a body
Weary though it was
Broken no more, returned to dust.

A weak warble draws your eye
Ashes sift as something moves

Deep within their depths
Something stirs back to life
Reaching in, you draw it forth
Tiny, naked, precious, newborn chick.

Within days it has regained itself.
Vibrant and full of life again.
Vivid plumage of ruby red,
Mixed with flaming orange and
Splashed with brilliant yellow.
Recalling to you the flames that birthed them.
Ash and Fire. Fire and Ash.
Rising from the ashes.
Phoenix of the flames.
Reborn. Renewed. Restored.

Dual Nature

Staring eyes
Twitching tail
Swiveling ears
Tensed body
A tiny killing machine
Is ready to pounce

Gaze fixed on the wall
Hearing sounds too faint
For your mere human ears
Waiting impatiently for the
Fatal, final mistake from their prey

Four legs of dense muscle
Capped with tiny toe beans
And razor sharp claws.
A mouth that yawns delicately,
Filled with serrated blades,
Otherwise known as teeth.
A body built to kill,
Waiting to do its job.

Soft fur.
Rough tongue.

Rumbling purrs.
Gentle kneading.
A tiny love machine
Is ready to cuddle.

Head butting your fingers,
Looking for scratches at the ears,
Long body stropping
Endlessly against your ankles,
Looking for a wee snack.

Silky tail curled around,
Tiny toe beans on display,
Vibrating deep within the chest
As you stroke from tip to tip.
Tongue swiping your hand,
Making biscuits on your leg.
A creature built to love,
Curled up on your lap.

Oma's Ode

You were the best.
You may say that isn't so,
but we are our own worst enemies.
Six children you raised,
for years all alone.
25 with out him, so few with.
But you got through it,
through 20 some years of adolescence
through 3 daughters marriages,
with 2 boys and a girl single still.
Through the birth of 6 grandkids,
you hoped to make one more.
Almost a graduation
almost a birth
almost a grandkid in college.
You came so close.
To soon we had to say goodbye.
To soon you left your earthly journey.
Now alone we go on
without you we travel.
Words can't explain how greatly I miss you.
They can't tell how much I still need you.
But they can tell you this
No matter what I still Love you.

All through my life know I'll miss you
remember what you taught me
and wish you still could
impart to me your advice and your wisdom.
But I guess the time has come
for me to accumulate my own wisdom
to come up with a bedrock to teach my own
grandchildren.
I hope that one day I will be just like you.
For no matter what you say,
you are the best woman ever
and my hero forever.
Love you, and miss you a million times over.

Gentleman's Drink

Sweet and fiery it slides down my throat;
golden amber in color it swirls in the glass;
cold in the bottle, warmed by my hands
liquid fire that serves to revive me.
The sweet taste is definitely acquired
but it is distinctive to the last drop.
Properly consumed it is warmed in a glass
by your life's' heat, through your hands.
A gentlemen's choice in days gone by
it rests on the mantel in a crystal decanter
sweet, fiery, golden gentlemen's brandy.

Music's Draw

The music plays
	haunting through the night.
The music echos
	playing through my soul.

The music leads
	to a deep internal peace.
The music drives
	the mind to deeper thought.

The music pulls
	through a mire of despair.
The music pushes
	to a place of great joy.

The music floats
	softly through the trees.
The music flies
	quickly to waiting ears.

The music impels
	me to seek the source.
The music draws
	me to where you are.

Shadow Lover Rescued

From the shadows release beckons cunningly.
It stands ready to free my soul from the world.
Tall, dark, hooded, cloaked he is a lover of
shadows.
In the darkness he hides preparing to strike.
Mostly by night, but occasionally by day he
works,
The lover of shadows calls me to him insistently,
Uttering sweet words, an impossible to ignore
call.
My first step to the dark is hesitant and unsure,
But they grow bolder, more confident in the
choice.
The shadow lover stands ready to embrace me to
him,
To welcome me to the darkness, the shadows he
haunts.
I take a step and reach out a hand to the
darkness,
So close to the shadows and my shadow lover I
stand.

His hand of ethereal darkness comes forth in
reply to mine,
His cold, leather bound fingers brush mine, but
then,
Before his hand can wrap itself about mine to
draw me in
A clamor comes from the light behind me,
directed at me.
The light, the noise cause my shadow lover to
cringe then run.
I turn to chastise my rescuer for his unwanted
help
And find myself arrested by the sight before me.
Slowly striding forth from the blinding light
If ever I thought my shadow lover was seductive
He compared in no way to this paragon of light.
Tall and fair with a shining cloak and a flaming
sword
He stood proud and assured in the blazing sun.
I hesitate to pour forth my recriminations
He seizes the chance to beckon me closer,
Away from the shadows, into the light.
Unknowingly, unthinkingly I follow the silent
order.
"The shadows are no place for a maid of such
beauty
the darkness would cover your fairness,
Death would glory in conquering your
loveliness."

"But death would not get me, I went not to him,
my shadow lover called, he beckoned me on
with words and actions he seduced to bring me
to him."
"Foolish maid, your shadow lover was Death,
from the darkness he seduces, fairness to
conquer."
"It was death that called me to his side? But
why?"
"You have much to offer him, a pearl of such
beauty,
but he merely wishes to conquer life, sees it as a
duty."
My savior took another step forward to me
His features settled into those of such
handsomeness
The face of an angel with a body to match.
As the thought crosses my mind I look at him
and gasp
An angel indeed or so the now unfurled wings
proclaim.
"I've done now my duty and I'll leave you with
this:
a lover will come to you and not from the
shadows,
a lover to give you what you thought Death
offered
a gift he will be from us above,
protect you from the shadows he will, and love."

With those words his wings beat and he rose
Up to the sky with his flaming sword and
shining cloak
Behind a cloud he disappeared and my thoughts
then cleared.
With one last glance at the shadows I walked on,
Content with my rescue and my promise.
A lover not of the shadows mine would be,
So with patience I wait for that gift from above.

Sunshine Bathed in Sunshine

Sunlight streams through the open window
bouncing through and illuminating your golden
tresses.
It shines across the hard, but softened planes of
your face
alternately highlighting and shadowing your
strong, masculine jaw.
The light bathes your whole self in a glow
picking out, making molten your already golden
skin.
The light shows clearly the troubles you have
suffered,
the gaunt lines in your face and the slightly
hollow belly,
a belly just visible above the sheet that covers
your lower half.
I feel terrible seeing the evidence of your
suffering
for I know I am its cause and that hurts.
I never meant to hurt you, to cause you pain.
I watch you, my sunshine, sleep, bathed in
sunshine.

You reach across to where I had been before
but when your hand finds nothing you wake.
Your deep brown eyes find my blue ones,
you walk to where I stand in the doorway,
tugging your tangled pants leg absentmindedly,
studying my face, my eyes, my soul.
With a possessive light in your eyes you capture
my lips
"I thought it was a dream," you whisper against
my lips,
"I thought I had lost you again, my heart
stopped."
"I'll never leave you again" I answer, "I
couldn't.
You are my sunshine bathed in sunshine."

Graceful Hands

Hands are such an amazing thing,
So expressive when they move,
And emphasizing the most important words.
Yours are more extraordinary then most,
Long, strong, rough, tender, handsome, manly.
Ready to wipe away my tears
To hold me close and comfort me.
Able to wield a knife, pen or instrument
With the most amazing of precision.
But will I ever to get to feel
Those gentle hands supporting me in my fear.
Or will I ever get to see
Those strong, rough hands defending me.
Or those long elegant hands performing
Some wonderfully intricate task.
Maybe someday I will be able
To hold and touch those wondrous hands
And be able to enjoy those hands holding me
Someday, hopefully one day
Your beautiful hands will belong to me
Along with your heart as mine is yours.

Life's Gift

Parental is the love
for our parents and
the love felt as a
parent for a child.

Familial is the
love for the rest
of our family,
siblings, cousins,
aunts, uncles, and
grandparents as well.
and the love we get
from them also.

Platonic is the love
for our friends. The
family that we choose.

Romantic is the love
we share with one
person forever.
It can lead to other
forms of love by itself.

Love is a precious

part of the most
miraculous gift of all.
The special gift we
all receive straight
from God for whom
we have the most
perfect type of love.
The gift of life.

Touch's Power

A touch
amazing how such a little thing
holds such power over us.
We crave the interaction,
we fear its harsher side.
We yearn for a caress,
we cringe from a slap.
A hug, a rub can make your day.
A smack or no touch at all can make you cry.
Even a pat, or the lightest contact
can brighten your whole day.

Our emotions are expressed by our touch.
Our emotions are soothed by the touch of others.
Each day we see hundreds of people,
some of them touch us, some of them don't.
Those that do we remember the most,
those that don't we forget real quick.
You might be touched by voice, actions, or
words,
but that which stands out most is the physical
touch.

Without physical contact we sink deep

deep into a realm of helplessness and despair
from which only tender care can save us.
We crave it like honey,
we shun it like a whip.
How powerful it is,
just a little touch.

Kitchen Thoughts

Sizzle. Pop. Fry.
Sweet smells fill the air.
A gentle melody rises from the pot.

Swish. Thunk. Cut.
Precise cuts divide the vegetables.
A careful pile fills the board.

Calculating eyes monitor the pot.
A practiced hand flashes the knife.
Mis en place ready for the next step.

Eyes review the recipe,
Preparing for those next steps.
Hands stir the fragrant mix.
Keeping it from burning.
Nose delights in the flavors,
Noting how they blend together.

The kitchen has its own dance.
Even if it is a ballet of one.
A home chef cooking for themselves.

A timer beeps somewhere.
Drawing immediate attention.

From the oven comes a pan.

The savory smell of roasted meat
The earthy smell of potatoes and carrots.
Resting on the counter.

A whisk begins to swirl
Running through and through
Flour and fat make a roux.
Add salt and pepper
Then the cooking liquid
To make a fabulous gravy.

Set it all in dishes fine.
Lay them on the table.
Call your guests to dine.

And when the savory is done
Pull forth that sweet pie
And let the praises come.

Worlds in the Stars

Stars twinkle high in the sky
Drawing up my eyes to their beauty
Taking my awareness from my mind
Capturing me in worlds far away.

Worlds in which peace exists for all
Places were none are judged or live unloved
Worlds were children know only security
And the happiness of being loved and protected.

Worlds where you can be yourself
Without a fear of recriminations
Where you don't have to hide behind normalcy
Where the thoughts of normal don't exist.

Worlds where people live as we should
Where people do not go against nature
Somewhere were war and poverty don't exist
Where no one dies of hunger or cold.

But a place like that is a dream
As such does it really exist?
Is it out there waiting to be found?
Waiting to teach us how to live?

Slowly I return my awareness to my mind
I come back from worlds of dreams
I come back from places beautiful
I reluctantly return to reality.

I bring my eyes back to our world
A world of violence, hate, war, despair
A place where you are judged, and not allowed
To exist as yourself, you must be normal.

Maybe one day our world will be better
Maybe it will be like the dream worlds
Love will exist for all in every way
Until then for it I will pray.

Beneath the Tree

Sunlight shines forth
      dappling the grass
      beneath the tree where we used to sit.

Wind blows softly
      stirring the grass
      beneath the tree where we used to sit.

Nuts thunk down
      speckling the grass
      beneath the tree where we used to sit.

Leaves float softly
      coloring the grass
      beneath the tree where we used to sit.

Snow quietly falls
      coating the grass
      beneath the tree where we used to sit.

Shoots poke forth
      becoming the grass
      beneath the tree where we used to sit.

Years pass by

changing the grass
      beneath the tree where we used to sit.

I come back to
      sit on the grass
      beneath the tree where we used to sit.

I wait for you to return
      always on the grass
      beneath the tree where we used to sit.

Music's Story

In the background a guitar softly strums.
I sit, curled up on the sofa, in the next room,
A book in my hand, thoughts in my mind.
From your room come the soft, sweet guitar
notes.

I let the music catch up my mind.
In its alluring net are my thoughts caught.
I drift freely in the web you unknowingly weave.
I float softly in the notes you lovingly play.

The quiet beauty of the notes is savored.
They inspire thoughts of peace, beauty and life.
A hope that it will never end enters my soul,
But then, all at once, the notes do indeed change.

The soft and smooth becomes hard and jarring.
The feelings of peace quickly dissipate.
In their place are feelings of anger and hate.
The quiet music is now music of anger and pain.

The anger is shocking in its intensity.
The pain is heartbreaking in its depth.
They overwhelm, killing any joy at all.
It threatens to drag you into an abyss of despair.

The dark notes continue on and on.
It seems as if it will go forever.
But I can feel it slightly lessening.
The music, it seems, serves as a catharsis.

Just as quickly as the jarring music began,
The music stops completely, silence prevails.
I am shocked back into myself by the lack.
Already I desire to hear the music once more.

After a moment the door to your domain opens.
You stand there with a face stonily impassive.
But now, I know your secret pain.
A pain I share, a pain that could bind.

For though I speak not of it,
Though I have never said a word,
I want there to be a bond between us.
I want you to know I care and have yours in
return.

They Gave All

A symbol of hope
 Within our hearts,
A sign of life
 To our eyes,
On the green hill
 Flowers grow free.
Behind the towering hill
 Graves lie quietly.

They stand for us
 As they fell.
The price of freedom:
 Some gave all.
Appropriately they lie there,
 Behind the hill.
So close to flowers
 Signs of hope.

They fell for us
 To be free.
To let us live.
Tall and strong
Even in the silence.
 Some gave all.

www.ingramcontent.com/pod-product-compliance
Lightning Source LLC
Chambersburg PA
CBHW070612160726
48003CB00005B/2233